Pain

Power

Purpose

**RELEASE, REGAIN,
AND REVEAL WHAT IS WITHIN**

BY

CAMEO THOMAS

Life Chronicles Publishing
Give your life a voice!

ISBN: 978-1-950649-56-3
Editor Michelle Anderl
Cover Layout: Life Chronicles Publishing
Life Chronicles Publishing Copyright © 2021
lifechroniclespublishing.com

TABLE OF CONTENTS

INTRODUCTION

Living a purposeful life is satisfying, but you can only do that once you have dealt with the pain of yesterday. Some people, while existing in the present, only live in the past. The mind and even the reality of each of these people are a reflection of their past. Therefore, they find it hard to move forward and explore the various opportunities the world offers. Undoubtedly, the past is a crucial piece of your life's puzzle. Everyone has a past, and sometimes, it can be the driving force of existence and living. However, when it becomes our present, it can leave us in ruins and shatters.

This book, *Pain — Power — Purpose*, is written to give hope to the hopeless and mend the lives of people who feel they are lost in this fast-paced world. It's designed to restore sanity to their life, help them to discover their true purpose on earth, and enable the pieces of themselves to coexist happily. Contrary to what you might think, it's possible beyond every reasonable doubt to live at peace with yourself and your past and to excel. There's always a light at the end of the tunnel, and although some people can't see it, this book will act as your guide. You can overcome your painful past and transform your life into one that would be a model for others.

The author, Cameo Thomas, is a life coach whose own life is an inspiration to thousands of people. Having overcome her traumatic past, Cameo Thomas decided to use her story to inspire people to not give up on life just yet and to live happily with themselves. Her passion is to help people live more purposefully and understand that they have the power to do anything they want to do.

Pain

Pain - Power - Purpose

Chapter One

MISSING PIECES

---

*"The Troubles of Yesterday Tend to
Follow Us in the Present, Hindering
Us from Reaching Our Pure
Potentiality, Yet Our Understanding of
it is Unknown to Us..."*

I was born in Portland in the 1980s to a black mother and a father of mixed races. I had all the love and care from my grandmother and great-grandmother, but my mother never seemed glad that I was born. Maybe she wished I was a boy so that she could get back with my father. Whatever her reason was for showing little love towards me was best known to her.

Exactly when I became five, I discovered that I had been born into the generational pain of being raised by a single parent. It was as if my life had been predestined. My mother was the only child of her parents' union, and she grew up knowing only her mother. My mother refused to move in with her father when he remarried, so she lived with her grandmother instead; that's where she met my father. I grew up with my grandmother and great-grandmother, just as my mother had grown up with hers. Maybe that was the reason for her hostility towards me—the pain of being left by my father after being abandoned by her own.

As I said earlier, my father was from a mixed race, and his adoptive family was white. My father's adoptive parents were a great family and treated him as if he were biologically theirs, like the daughter they had before adopting him. It was not until my father became an adult that he requested to see his biological parents. They were still very much alive at that time.

My parents were teenagers messing around, not knowing that bringing a child into this world would be a responsibility that they were not equipped for. Their childhood trauma played a role in how they did and did not parent my siblings and me—my father being adopted, and my mother abandoned by her mother and left to be raised by her alcoholic father and his parents.

I grew up across the street from my childhood elementary school, which was both a blessing and a curse. I can remember attending Martin Luther King Jr. Elementary School and my classmates being dropped off and picked up at school by their mothers or fathers. Me, I was being picked up by my great-grandmother. Sometimes, she or my great-grandfather just watched from the front porch, waiting for me to dodge cars and school buses to get across. There were moments I wondered where my parents were. Why didn't they walk me to school? Why didn't they pick me up from school? My mom was always working, and when she finally moved out and got her own place (in an apartment building for low-income families), she would drop me off in the mornings at my great-grandparents house, and I would go to school from there. It was the same thing after school; she would still be at work, unable to pick me up. My father was in and out of my life, and although I knew of him, I did not really know him. I can remember him coming to my great-grandparents' house to see me, and I would run upstairs. I can also remember those times when he promised my mom that he was coming to pick me up, and my excitement kept me in front of that big window facing Martin Luther King Jr. Elementary School. I would sit at that large window for hours, waiting and watching people walk and bike by, cars drive past, and my great-grandfather's friends hang out in the front of the house. All the while, I was still waiting for my father to come pick me up. My great-grandmother would watch the excitement on my face turn to sadness. I remember asking her, "Grandmama, why didn't he come get me? He said he was coming to get me." Her response was always, "Baby, I don't know, but let's go outside and I will watch you ride your bike." She would stay on the front porch, watching me ride my pain away on my purple and pink bike. This would go on throughout my childhood, and it affected me in ways that built walls around my heart and kept me from trusting others.

My mother was an alcoholic for most of my childhood and early adult life. I remember being left at home at the age of nine with my baby brother for an entire day. One morning, she said she was leaving to go grocery shopping and did not return until that night. How could she do this to me? How could she leave me here at home with a four-month-old baby? This was the day I learned how to make a baby's formula bottle, change a dirty diaper, and make noodles in the microwave. She returned home with no groceries, just the slurred speech she yelled at me for questioning her about where she had been.

The abuse soon followed. I remember asking simple questions like, Where are we going? and Are you coming back to get us? My question would be answered with a slap in the face, push to the floor, beating with a belt. The abuse would happen when she was either drinking or mad at one of her boyfriends, or better yet, the father of her children. It didn't stop there but got worse and even began to happen in public. I can remember going to the corner store on 42nd and

Prescott. She gave me the money to run in and grab her a Pepsi. "Hurry up and come right out!" she yelled. That's exactly what I did, except I grabbed a Diet Pepsi by accident, and that's when she punched me in my left eye. I cried and got hit even more for it. "You better stop crying before I give you something else to cry about." This phrase was oh-so common from her mouth. "You better not tell anybody I hit you, or I'm gone beat yo ass!" Even though my mother provided the basics— food, shelter, and clothing—there was more that I needed. I questioned myself, Why was she so mad at me? What did I possibly do wrong? I gazed into the sunny sky, getting myself together and trying to cover my eye with my long bangs as we headed to my great-grandparents' house.

By the time I was in middle school, I had endured emotional, mental, and physical abuse from my mother. My dad came around at his convenience. The only consistent people I had in my life were my great-grandparents and grandparents, until one day I met a lady at my cousin's house while playing over there. A man came through the door and I ran up to him yelling, "Daddy," and he picked me up. The lady was in shock, saying, "Oh, this is your daughter?" "Yep," my dad replied. The lady was my cousin's mom's friend and dating my dad at the time. Surprise! She also had a daughter that was a few years younger than me and that I inherited as a sister. As they continued dating, I would spend more time with the lady, her daughter, and her nieces than with my dad. I was receiving the love and nurturing that I didn't know I needed. This woman took care of me like I was her biological daughter. At one point, she, her daughter (eventually my sister), and I took pictures together like a family. My sister and I even had matching hairstyles.

Although my father was in and out of my life, he instilled in me this mantra: "Don't let nobody see you stress, and don't show no love especially to the opposite sex." Now you may wonder, "What? Didn't he have a girlfriend, and didn't he show love to her? Didn't she treat you like her own?" Yes, and I even began to call her Mom and refer to her as my stepmom. However, my dad would never make it official, even after having two kids, my younger sister and brother, from their unofficial union. During their relationship, my dad cheated and had another baby, my youngest sister, with another woman. I can remember so vividly riding in the car with my dad down North Interstate Street wondering as a nine-year-old, "Where the heck are we going? This is not Northeast Portland!" As we pulled into a parking spot and began to get out of the car, I noticed that we were in an unfamiliar place and it didn't feel right, but hey, I'm with my dad so it's all good. We walked through a door and down a hallway that smelled like mothballs—ugh! Then we walked up some loud, squeaky stairs where it felt like we were about to be grabbed, like in the movie *The People Under the Stairs*. We got to the top and my dad knocked on the door. A woman opened it. I followed my dad in and sat on the couch next to him. The woman sat down across from us and smiled while saying "Hi" to me. She was pretty, with beautiful hair, and she kind of reminded me of my mom with the smile. My dad introduced her to me as his friend, they chatted for a few more minutes, and then we left. As we were walking down the stairs, my dad said to me, "Don't tell anybody we were here." I never told my stepmom, but I for sure told my mom.

Two years later at a family gathering and after the transition of a family member, my aunt told me to come to her because she had someone for me to meet. As soon as I walked in the house, there was the woman I met two years before at the house I went to with my dad. She was holding a baby girl. My aunt said to me, "Niecey, this is your baby sister." At the time, I was excited because I loved babies, but I also felt confused. She looked just like me when I was a baby, light skin, fat, and no hair, but without the green eyes. I held her and played with her outside on the front porch, then gave her back to her mom once she started to cry. Why didn't my dad disclose this to me? Why didn't either of my mothers tell me this?

Every single event we experienced during our childhood, whether rough or smooth, forms a huge part of our adulthood. You can't become an adult without passing through life's phases—childhood, adolescence, and the teenage stage. Have you ever tried putting together a puzzle that someone gave you and discovered that putting the pieces together wasn't as easy as you thought it would be? How do you approach it then?

First, you come up with a strategy. You start off with the easy pieces—the outer straight sides. Good! You are making progress. Your strategy is working, and you even hype yourself by saying that it's easy. But as you begin to move inward to get to the center of the puzzle, it becomes more complicated to put the pieces together. Did you really expect it to be that easy? You even later discover that some of the pieces were missing or lost and that was the reason the pieces didn't fit correctly. Now that you have discovered this, what then? Will you walk away or continue to fight to complete the puzzle?

Most of the time, we get frustrated when we are challenged, and the next thing that comes to our mind is to walk away from the situation. We give up and don't attempt again to figure it out. The simple fact is that it requires patience, perseverance, and attention to find those pieces that will fit right.

Every day we work with our past experiences and the people in our lives to put the right pieces together and complete the puzzle. What's this puzzle? Your life is the puzzle. Every piece in this puzzle represents something concrete that happened in your life. The goal here isn't to overthink or live in the past, it's to learn from your life experiences and figure out where each piece fits in your present life and even your future.

My life hasn't been the most fun out there. My childhood especially was full of numerous sad moments and a few happy moments. Having to deal with an alcoholic and abusive mother and an absent father, I learned to be a somewhat independent, resourceful leader despite being just a nine-year-old girl then. But did these lessons break me or turn me into who I am today? I owe my life and everything to what I passed through, and knowing more about God helped to discover my life's purpose. Let me say this: we are more than capable of taking control of our lives, even when life knocks us down. We all have followed the popular assumption that time heals all wounds, but real life doesn't reflect this. It's what we do with our time that changes us. Do you choose to live in the past or focus on the future? Do you choose to make the changes that will move you forward or let past experiences knock you around like a soccer ball, turning you into what you never wanted to become? The choice is yours.

Chapter Two

UNSEEN PAIN

"*Pain is temporary,*
quitting lasts forever."
—*Lance Armstrong*

At age eleven, just finishing fifth grade, I lost a cousin to gun violence and found out that my dad cheated on my stepmom and had a baby. Straight confusion. I really didn't know how to process it. I went to my dad and stepmom's house that night and cried nonstop for hours over the death of my cousin that I looked up to. A few days later, my dad, stepmom, two little sisters, and I were on a flight to Los Angeles to visit Disneyland. I put meeting my new baby sister in the back of my mind and didn't tell either one of them that I had met her or even knew about the cheating. We enjoyed Disneyland as the family that I always wanted. The sunny weather, the togetherness, the love was everything I needed, and I never wanted it to end. Returning back to Portland was bittersweet, and transitioning to middle school was full of the unexpected.

As I began middle school, I dealt with issues at home by being very focused on my schoolwork. I would lock myself in my room, textbooks open, music blasting through my headphones from the discman playing either 2Pac's "Me Against the World" or Silkk's "The Shocker: Charge It 2 Da Game." Then on the other hand, at school I was dealing with teasing and bullying. Here I was, very light skinned—too much melanin for some and not enough for others, standing 4'11", very skinny and weighing 100 pounds. While the girls around me were blossoming, I was still flat chested with a butt as flat as a wall. I was teased and called "Skin and Bones" by peers, while family members called me "Skinny Minnie" and "Mello Yellow." I took it all in but kept pushing on. I soon began to only hang around boys and was sort of a tomboy. I dressed in the newest Fila Grant Hills, K-Swiss Classics, and Pumas and would rock these with a full tracksuit or denim skirt. By seventh grade, things began to look up at home with my mom, so I thought. She had a new boyfriend that she ended up marrying after six months of dating. Her attention was less on abusing me and my brother than on her new man. While she continued to provide food and shelter, I was still missing something from her. I began selling and smoking weed. I would even smoke with my stepdad. He said he would rather have me and my friend smoke with him because it was safer. Yeah, I know, how safe is that to smoke with your stepdad? I began getting into fights at school, suspended, and almost expelled by the time I left eighth grade. My grades and respect towards my teachers were the only things that kept me in school. If I had failing grades, I for sure would have been expelled, and only God knows how much worse these years would've been.

As humans, it's perfectly okay to feel pained. However, how we express it and channel it matters. Most of the time, we channel our pain into doing stupid and negative things. The pain of not getting that motherly love, coupled with the school bullying and teasing, put me in a bad emotional state that almost cost me my education. It led me to almost commit a blunder that would have ruined my life for good. I knew that I didn't have the relationship with my mom that most daughters have with their mothers, but I felt pained that she was going to abandon me and my younger brother once she left with a man. Everyone deserves motherly love, and I was afraid that I would be deprived of that. Those pains remained with me throughout seventh grade, but I was able to overcome them.

Because I was so young then, I thought the only way to feel belonging and channel all my pain and suffering was to do the thing that my friends were doing—smoking. At that time, I felt like I really didn't fit in with the different crowds at school. So, what did I do? I got mixed up with friends that influenced me both positively and negatively. Selling and smoking weed came at the height of my frustration during high school.

The association made me coldhearted. I was always fighting and angry with myself. It was a bad idea, and that was reflected in my academics and my relationship with my teachers. I was a good student, but I realized that if I didn't do something urgently, I would lose the only thing that I derived joy from—school.

When you have an unseen pain rooted inside you, there's only one thing you can do to prevent it from getting in your way—channel it into doing positive things. That includes activities that you love and feel happy doing. If you keep your pain buried, it will manifest in a surprising way that you will regret. The worst thing is that it will happen when you least expect it, and you will definitely have minimal control over it.

I overcame the death of my cousin, the remarriage of my mother, the bullying and teasing, and the smoking by channeling my emotions into studying. I told myself that it was best to put at bay everything regarding the past that could affect me in school. It worked incredibly well.

Your past experiences can ignite anger, increase your stress levels, and plant all sorts of things in your head. Repeated events can also ignite negative emotions that may be hard to control. The worst part is that your negative emotions can become habits that will infiltrate your normal living. You become a slave to these emotions, and when this happens, you become easily annoyed and bitter with people. On top of this, your natural defense mechanism is to respond with anger. You need to transform your unseen pain into something good and worth living for.

Remember, the only way you can control your pain is by channeling it into doing something positive. However, before you do that, you need to first and foremost deal with the negative emotions and anger that arise from this unseen pain buried inside of you. To do this, you have to follow the steps below:

Stop Justifying

Stop justifying getting upset each time you recall those unforgettable moments of pain. You and you only have the power to stop this. Do you want to be like that person that tells everyone they met how awful life is? How life sucks? If you stop justifying the need to get angry and negative, you have just crossed the first bridge in channeling your anger and pain.

Stop Creating Socially Acceptable Explanations for Your Actions and Behavior

The next step is to stop making excuses for yourself and others. Accept your life's mistakes and that of the other person that you feel has wronged you. You may try to verbalize your anger and create explanations for your behavior or pain. Either way, it's not helping. If you don't let go of this, you will be giving negative emotions the chance to control you and make you miserable. Learn to move past that.

Take Full Responsibility

Now that you have stopped inventing excuses to justify your actions and behavior, it's high time that you take responsibility for yourself. Once you do this, negative emotions and anger lose their hold over you. Taking responsibility for your actions is part of being an adult. So, act like one.

Don't Give People Power Over You

The fact is, it can be complicated to control your anger and pain if you are surrounded by people that keep reminding you of them one way or the other. People can be jerks and can use a piece of information that they know about you to taunt you and define your image. Don't let anyone do that to you. You are the only person that can define your worth. If you give people your power and allow them to tell you who you are, you are likely to react angrily. You will then feel inferior, embarrassed, and ashamed to the extent that you will resort to self-pity. But when you stop allowing people to define you, you will become much happier.

Declutter Your Bad Habits

Discard anything and everything that makes you feel bad and remember the awful things that happened to you in the past. It may be difficult to do, but there's no way around it. If you must make that shift and move towards positive actions, you need to eliminate those bad habits. To eliminate those habits, figure out the people that influence you both positively and negatively, and filter out the negative ones. Habits of people close to you are highly influential, and bad ones can induce negative thinking. By reducing this, your pain becomes lighter.

Don't Limit Yourself

Saying things like, "I can't let go," is one way of affirming that you will continue to let the pain of yesterday hunt you forever. It means that you will continue to make room for those negative emotions to keep growing. At some point in my life, I felt like giving up my family and quitting everything because I had affirmed that I couldn't let go of all the things I had experienced. Then I thought of the future and my kids. I wouldn't let my marriage just go down the drain—I didn't want to take care of my children alone and go through divorce like my parents. And yes, I said, "I can do it." I can live a normal life and grow old with my husband and children.

The only reason you believe that you can't move beyond your past is because you already have it in your mind that you can't. The power of doing lies within you. Stop limiting what you can do. You can if you say so.

USING THE MIND TO CONTROL YOUR UNSEEN PAIN

Pain involves both the mind and the body. The pain from the inside always stems from past experiences, and this can affect the mind and body in ways that you can't ever foresee. Therefore, the use of mind-body therapies is an ideal solution.

Mind-body therapies have the capacity to keep your emotions in check, alleviate pain, and change your lifestyle for good. They also change the way you perceive the world and inoculate you with new ideas and values. So, while your brain is wired to the events of the past and the pain from those experiences, introducing mind-body therapies can do magic. The impressive thing about these therapies is that they are painless, easy, and effective, and you can practice a combination of one or two techniques for an even greater effect.

Let's look at some of these techniques.

Deep Breathing

Deep breathing is the simplest of all mind-body techniques. Yet it's the first one that you must learn, as it's central to all other techniques. To practice deep breathing, inhale a large breath and hold it for a few seconds before exhaling. To help relieve pain, you can use two words—one that you would love to take into your life and the other that you want to let go of. For instance, you can breathe in "peace" and breathe out "sadness."

Meditation

The importance of meditation in our lives is beyond incredible. Each day, preferably after sunrise, begin the day with meditation. Practice deep breathing while paying attention to each breath. Back it up with some calm music and picture yourself in a restful environment, full of flowing waters.

Mindfulness

Deep breathing is used here again. While breathing deeply, pay attention to each breath to become fully immersed in it. You can pick any activity that you love for this practice. Notice every detail and record how your senses and emotions are responding.

Yoga

Yoga incorporates physical exercise, breathing, and meditation. It's a mind-body technique that stretches and strengthens the muscles and other parts of the body, relieving them of tension and pain. Yoga classes are available online and offline. There are a wide range of apps that can get you started.

Positive Thinking

You can become fixated on your pain if you think about it repeatedly. How about shifting from thinking about pain to thinking more positively? Retrain your mind to think of the things that you can do instead of what you can't. Positive thinking opens your mind to a new world of endless possibilities. With that, you become aware that there are a lot of things that you can do to help out yourself, the community, and the world at large.

We all experience that unseen pain from time to time. As humans, we can't eradicate it completely because there are a lot of things that may trigger them. However, you can put the pain at bay by not focusing too much on them. Don't pretend that they don't exist. Rather, acknowledge them and look for ways to make yourself feel better. If making yourself better means seeking out help from experts, friends, family members, or others, then do it.

Pain - Power - Purpose

Chapter Three

WHOM DO YOU LOVE?

*"The best and most beautiful things in
the world cannot be seen or even
heard, but must be felt with the heart."*
—Helen Keller

In my twenties, I was more of a people pleaser and allowed others to have a strong influence on who I should be and how I should act. I was always doing what others wanted me to do or expected of me, and this continued even after I got married to my husband. Neither he nor I knew how to be the so-called perfect spouse, and we projected our expectations on one another but never acknowledged or learned the expectations we had for ourselves.

I did almost everything my husband demanded of me. As a faithful wife and a God-fearing lady, I obeyed without questions. I loved him immensely, being that he was my first, but I didn't notice we had issues. Two years into our marriage and after having three children, my husband cheated on me. Initially, I became furious. I mean, why would he cheat on me, despite giving him all my love and being a good wife and mother? I forgave him, but it didn't stop there. He cheated on me again with his side chick and got her pregnant. He even moved out of the home, leaving me to cater to my three children. Call it déjà vu.

Was I wrong for loving my husband the way I did or did not? Maybe I lacked something, and he was too scared to let me know. Maybe I didn't give him the attention that he wanted, and he decided to seek it elsewhere. At that time, I was busy with work, but didn't last long on any job because I didn't find any of them fulfilling. Sometimes I had doubts that he didn't love me the way I loved him. Today, this sentence has been the bane of relationships and cause of break-ups and divorces.

Some couples no longer share the same level of love they had when they met the first time. Why do you think this is? Couples no longer engage in activities that will foster love and care.

Relationships and marriages require more than just loving your partner or being loved. That deep connection that you develop from doing activities together is what strengthens the relationship. These days, we are so busy with work and the bustle of life that we no longer spend as much time as we used to with our spouses and partners. Whom do you love more? Your career or your spouse? When such questions are brought up, couples tend to get involved in an altercation that usually leaves them on the brink of a divorce or separation. This is where cheating and other marriage vices stem from because both partners couldn't lay their guards down. But divorce isn't always the answer. Sometimes, separation, individual and couples counseling may assist in repairing the relationship. During my marital crisis, my husband and I had our pastor counsel us, and eventually, we reconciled.

It doesn't matter how busy you are at your office; you can still make time for your partner. You don't have to work long hours. The little things that we often ignore have almost the same impact as the big ones we tend to cherish. While you focus on creating more time to be with your partner, you need to also work on yourself. Develop those areas that you feel you are lacking in. Pay more attention to your health, body, and emotions. Focus on growing stronger and better. When you start to love yourself, your partner will be in awe of you and love you more.

Choose to love yourself, your partner and find ways to make them feel comfortable the best way you can, regardless of the nature of your job. Strike a balance between spending time with them and with your work. If you are unable to make it home early, keep in constant communication with your partner. This will prevent them from being unnecessarily worried.

Chapter Four

I ACKNOWLEDGE YOU

> *"Do unto your partner as your*
> *partner would like you to do"*
> —*John Van Epp*

Acknowledging your partner is one of the things that strengthens a relationship. It shows that you don't only care about them but appreciate their efforts and what they do. The good thing is you can show your partner that you care without spending a lot of money. You don't need a fancy vacation, nor do you need to make a public declaration to make your bond more solid. Acknowledging your partner involves doing little things and showing spontaneous acts of kindness that express how much they mean to you. Acts, words, gifts, and touches are some of the meaningful things that partners desire- as written by author Gary Chapman.

What is the importance of acknowledging your partner? It will let your partner know that they are doing a good job. Couples relate to each other based on feedback, and the only way to know that your partner is doing what you love is to acknowledge them. What can you acknowledge your partner for? You can comment on how attractive they are, how fantastic they are at cooking, or how caring they are as a partner. If you wish to express a negative comment, do that constructively so that they don't feel bad.

What are the meaningful ways you can show appreciation to your partner and acknowledge them for who they are? Below are some of them:

Sending a Special Gift

Sending gifts may be a common way of showing how much you value your partner, but it's one act that's priceless. You can mail your partner a love letter, send them flowers, buy them a lovely shirt, or gift them their favorite candy.

Show Them That They Are Never Alone

One of the greatest things you can do for your partner is let them know that they are never alone in whatever decision they make. If they enroll in a music class, even if you don't really enjoy music, accompanying them will mean a lot and show that you support their decision. This way, you are acknowledging them and making them feel more appreciated.

Leave a Love Note

Couples can express love to their partners by placing a handwritten love letter in their lunch bag or on the nightstand before bed. These little gestures show how appreciative you are of them.

Doing Household Chores

Sometimes, couples decide to divide the chores between each other so that each person helps out. However, you can show how much you care by stepping in when your partner is too tired. This not only shows that you love them, but it also shows that you acknowledge and respect them.

Give Them a Warm Embrace

Make it a point to greet your partner at home with a kiss and a hug. This act connects the two of you, and in moments like this, it shows that your partner is your top priority and that you are glad that they arrived home safely.

Prepare Breakfast

This may seem common, but it shows a great deal of love and affection. Preparing breakfast for your partner before they wake up shows that you are thinking of them and that you would want them to feel super-comfy and prepared for the day's tasks. If you can bring them breakfast in bed, especially when you know that they are tired, they will feel truly loved and will respect you.

There are tons of ways you can acknowledge your partner and make them feel special. As earlier stated, you don't need to acknowledge them in expensive ways. The options mentioned here are enough to show that you value them and support what they are doing. **Acknowledge Your Partner Today!**

Chapter Five

I CHOOSE ME

"It's not selfish, but selfless to be first, to be as good as possible to you, to take care of you, to keep you whole and healthy. That doesn't mean that you disregard everything and everyone, but you gotta keep your cup full."
— Iyanla Vanzant

At some point in my life, I felt like I was living under the shadow of other people. I allowed people to dictate how I should live my life and how I had to do certain things. This gave me the impression that I had no purpose—that I would continue to live my life in the image of what others thought I should be. This was back in seventh grade, when I started to do the things my friends were doing just to feel like I belonged.

Unfortunately for us, there's no guide on how we should each live our lives. That would be too straightforward and boring, right? We have to learn what our mission on earth is through our bad and good experiences. However, you should never make the mistake of living for others and taking care of them while forgetting to take care of yourself. Make your mantra, **I choose myself.**

What does "choosing yourself" mean? It means living your life for no one else, not even your family or closest friend. It's living for you and you only. Choosing yourself means you are dancing to the tune of your song and are determined to live by it—you are accepting the life that you have.

Choosing yourself means deciding to maintain positive energy around you and allow no room for any form of negativity. It means setting standards in your life. No matter what, you don't deviate from them. You have to make a decision to always love yourself above everyone else. This doesn't mean that you shouldn't trust other people, but it simply means that you are accountable to yourself. A lot of people ask if choosing yourself is selfish. The answer is "No," although quite a number of people would say "Yes." That's because they don't understand what loving yourself entails. When you decide to love yourself, you are saying that you care about yourself enough to let go of the things that could cause you stress and depression. It doesn't mean that you are disrespecting others or that you don't care about them. It means that you don't want to get stuck always maintaining other people's sanity while abandoning your own issues. This is crucial to maintaining your sanity and emotional state. Choosing yourself is not selfish in any way.

When you choose yourself, it means that you don't depend on anyone else for your happiness. You have everything that you need in yourself. You are in control of your life, not influenced by other people's opinions. Choosing yourself allows you to live to your full potential because you do the things that you love and enjoy. You can do anything that you put your mind to and are motivated to go the distance for. Most importantly, choosing yourself helps you to know your worth and become the best version of yourself.

Putting your needs before those of others and making yourself your top priority is the only way you can thrive in this world. You can only know yourself in and out, while knowing so much about others is impossible. This is the only way to correctly determine who you are. You can't live by the rules of other people. Yes, it will take some practice to learn to put yourself first; it might sound scary at first, and you may even get some things wrong. However, this is the only way to know yourself better and become familiar with your body's responses and understand what it needs.

Even when it seems like your decision might hurt others, I'm certain that you will never be sorry for going in this direction. I have been in several positions where I put the needs of others before mine, and in the end, I either ended up hurting myself or getting the other person hurt. The truth is you can't know what's best for someone else (except probably for an infants and small children). You can only know what's best for you, so choose you. In the same way, no one else can know what's right for you. Unfortunately, that includes your parents.

Sometimes, we may find ourselves in a complex situation, and so we seek some advice from friends, family, and authority figures on what to do or how to proceed. This isn't bad, but the power to make decisions is right within your body. Most of the time, our bodies send us signals, but we often don't pay attention to them because our minds are clouded. We are always absorbed in our thoughts and experiences. In order to notice the signals and take appropriate action, you need to place more credence in your feelings—you need to listen more to your body and stop drowning in your thoughts. Always trust what your body tells you because it never lies. This is what I call mindfulness.

When something isn't right, you should pay attention to your body's sensations rather than the thoughts in your head. It doesn't matter how many reasons you come up with to choose one way or the other. If your body feels heavy when you think about it, then you should drop it.

If it's right, your body will feel light and lean towards the feeling of expansion. This is how to use the body's sensations and make life-changing decisions. You can use this knowledge to pick one awful experience you've had and then do the same for the thing that you absolutely loved. Close your eyes and pay attention to your body. You will notice how your body reacts to these memories.

Make yourself your top priority. Feel good, and stop worrying excessively about the feelings of other people. You can't know how deeply they feel. Remember that your mind will tell you otherwise, but don't let it fool you. Your body is what you should pay maximum attention to. Rather than worry so much about how another person feels, teach them how to value and take care of themselves. Choose yourself, and life will become more beautiful, blissful, and enjoyable.

Power

Pain - Power - Purpose

Chapter Six

IT'S TIME

> *"Learn from yesterday,*
> *live for today, hope for tomorrow."*
> *—Albert Einstein*

At some points in my life, I felt stagnant and unable to move past my demons and all that I had experienced, from my childhood to adulthood. This is because I was still holding onto some of them. My emotions were linked to those events that seriously impacted my life because those experiences caused me so much pain and suffering. After each time my husband hurt me, for instance, when he cheated on me, I would bring up the topic over and over again, and I used those incidents to punish him, even when he was genuinely sorry for his transgressions. Eventually, these affected my progress and career, and that's when I realized that the only way to grow was to let go and draw closer to God. It was time that I put certain things behind me for good—talk about burying the hatchet! I focused on being happy and above all, I learned to forgive.

In life, one of the most difficult things is letting go of those events that are irrelevant to you and letting go of those things that won't contribute anything meaningful to your present and future. These events will only make you sad and full of regret. There are several things that can impact your perspective; experiences can change you. That change will occur, even though you may not be ready for it. You feel tired of life, of everything, and at some point, you feel helpless. Maybe you can't handle that trying period in your relationship or career, and at last you decide to just give up on life because you no longer see any reason to exist. No! There's always a better way.

The question you need to ask yourself is how you can get back on your feet and free yourself from the clutches of your past. How can you stand strong and walk on solid ground? How can you put the pieces of your life back together and move forward? It's common for everyone to experience trying times at various points in life. You must experience that dark part, but will you allow it to have full control over you? Falling is part of life, but your ability to stand up again is what defines you. That's where the victory lies.

I had to come to terms with a lot of things before I could move forward. Whether you like it or not, accepting the hurt and disappointments is the first step towards progress. Accepting doesn't mean that you are ignoring these events; it simply means that you have decided to approach those painful experiences differently and are now on your way towards psychological and physical healing.

What are those things that are holding you back? Is one your failed relationship or marriage? Your career? Why can't you get over them, and why must you move beyond them? Ask yourself if holding on to these hurtful experiences will change the trajectory of your life and influence you positively. Answering these questions will give you a clear sense of purpose and help you stay committed to letting go.

You also need to identify your emotional habits, and this will require deep introspection. Does your past allow you to live normally? When you grow accustomed to certain emotions, you don't really take note of how they impact your living. You don't notice that you are stuck in a negative emotional loop, even when your reactions to certain situations say it all. You need to identify your emotional habits and start to shift towards a more positive experience. Your emotions function like the way your muscles work—you can train them. You can train yourself to feel sad or frustrated, and at the same time, you can train yourself to feel happy, passionate, and strong when challenges arise. When you take charge of your emotions, it will be easier to let go of your past and all of your sad experiences. You will come to feel lighter and freer.

You must learn to condition your mind as well. The more you train the mind, the more you are able to control your emotions and adapt to any situation that may arise. But what does it take to condition the mind? The breakthroughs that happen in life occur as a result of learning and following strategies and ensuring that you are in the right state of mind to move forward. To achieve this, you need to take time to change your habits. If you don't, life will just happen to you, and you will have no control over certain situations in your life. No matter how tactful, smart, or savvy you may be, if you don't build a barricade to obstruct your past from influencing your life's goals and decisions, then you are surrendering yourself to failures. Change your habits by empowering your mind with success stories and positive vibes. Feed your mind with new knowledge that revolve around achieving life's goals. Work at making your mind a thriving garden instead of patches of weeds.

Speaking of cultivating a thriving garden, you should establish empowering rituals. Letting go of the past is difficult, and that's why creating empowering rituals is important. It's the small practices that you do every day that will bring about massive changes to your life. What are these empowering rituals? Meditation, waking up early, exercise, eating healthily, and not missing breakfast are daily routines that you should incorporate into your life.

I counsel people who struggle with practicing gratitude and establishing routines that would help their lives. Instead, some prefer to live in the past. I tell them that practicing gratitude can help them realize that everything they have undergone in the past is what has shaped them in their present life. It's difficult to forget the past, but you can choose not to live in it. How do you practice gratitude? Start a gratitude journal—think about all that you have to be grateful for in your life and jot it down. Also, when you show self-love, it will be easier to let go of the past.

Now that you have accepted your past, what's next? You need to pick up some lessons. In other words, you need to distinguish the positive aspects of your painful past experiences. We are nothing without our past, but that doesn't mean that our past should negatively impact our decisions and life's goals. By learning from past experiences, you understand certain things about your existence, what makes you happy and what doesn't. For instance, what lessons did you pick up from your last break-up? What lessons did you learn from being constantly beaten by your parents and teachers? If you didn't learn anything, then you need to sit down and go over them again. Learning new lessons is vital to moving forward.

You can give yourself permission to let go of the unimportant people and memories, process, and take a cue from those hurtful moments. Sometimes, this can be difficult, but you don't have a choice. It can be complicated trying to process a sad event, but learning from it and focusing on creating the life that you want will provide you with closure and help you to move forward with your life. You can use these experiences to your advantage and learn how to grow. It can take days, weeks, or even months before you learn, but you need to move beyond the pain of yesterday that has been holding you back. **It's Time**!

Often, we sabotage our happiness by convincing ourselves that we don't have what it takes to be happy.

For instance, rather than allowing yourself to mingle and find a new friend that could become a potential soul mate, you question whether you possess the elements that would make them like you. "What if they refuse to associate with me?" The "what ifs" become more ingrained in your head than the positive possibility of having new friends around. At that moment, you retreat.

You have to start allowing yourself to let go of guilt and self-doubt and to seize every opportunity that may make you happy or positively influence your life. You shouldn't allow your anger and fear of the future to keep you trapped in the past. If there are people who have wronged you in the past, allow yourself the chance to forgive them. Forgive yourself for the moments when you messed up too. When you forgive, you are allowing yourself the space to move on, love yourself more, and take control of your life. One of the reasons my mind kept going back to past trauma, despite affirming that I was letting go, was that I kept playing the victim in my head. I was thinking that the bad experiences of my past were due to my mistakes and failures. These memories kept haunting me, and soon my mind became plagued by them. It was almost impossible for me to live beyond the past with this victim mindset.

Eventually, I stopped playing the victim because I realized that I was in control of my fate, and everyone has the right to control their own life. Just because I made a mistake or failed doesn't mean that I'll repeat it again. I stopped being the victim, and instead, I acknowledged my mistakes and tried to improve myself. You should do the same. It's wrong to blame yourself for your failures and mistakes, whether you were responsible for them or not. Be the survivor instead of the victim.

In a relationship or marriage, if it was the other person that wronged you, the best thing to do is to forgive and forget. You shouldn't wait for them to make an apology. It might take forever, and waiting only means that you will keep yourself in bondage and deprive yourself of love and happiness. Oprah Winfrey once said, "True forgiveness is when you can say, 'Thank you for the experience.'" Waiting for that apology won't help you. Forgive and focus on moving on from the past.

Many people have an affinity for drinking, smoking, or eating junk food. In fact, the idea of stopping these habits sound too intimidating and nearly impossible. These are not healthy habits, and in the long run, they will suffer from the consequences. Even though they know that these habits are bad, they don't have the drive to stop. I felt this same exact way when I smoked weed during my high school days. Truthfully, it's somewhat impossible to stop ourselves from doing certain things, even if it has a negative impact on us. However, two things can help you conquer them—willpower and determination. If you are determined to stop, your willpower will act accordingly. The same goes for your past. If you want to let go, you have the power to do so. Pick up what's leftover and move forward.

Accepting your past, learning from it, and moving on creates a new vision of the future. If you dwell on your past experiences and negative circumstances, you'll hardly think of the future, and this is sad because the future is more important than your past. Moving on creates a mental image of a bright, successful future.

Now that you have decided to move forward, it's time to focus on developing yourself. It's time to know yourself better and get on with doing things that will make you happy. Go out and participate in new activities. Surely you have a passion for something. Do things that will make you appreciate yourself. Spend time with yourself and learn to treat yourself with love. There's more on self-love in the next chapter.

Above all, learn to live in the present. Buddha said, "The secret of health for both mind and body is not to mourn for the past, worry about the future, or anticipate troubles, but to live in the present moment wisely and earnestly." In simple words, Buddha is telling us to enjoy the present because that's where we currently are. Each second, minute, or hour that passes never comes back again, so why waste the opportunity to make good use of it? If you are struggling to redirect your body and mind to the present, try some mindfulness and meditation practice.

Even when you have succeeded in letting go, I must say that you will face setbacks and challenges. A lot of events that will happen in the future will remind you of your past, but if you remain strong and focused, it is unlikely that you will be affected. The best thing you can do for yourself is to focus on the present and not the past. The past doesn't define who you are, but whatever decision you make in the present affects your future. Focus on the present moment and leave the past in the past.

Chapter Seven

LOVE THYSELF, HEAL THYSELF

---

*"Love yourself first and
everything else falls into line."*
—Lucille Ball

Everyone witnesses a devastating period at some point in their lives. I witnessed mine in childhood and when I was a teenager, but the events of those periods didn't stop me from being who I am. I developed and learned from all the mistakes I made. When my husband cheated on me, I thought I did something wrong to piss him off along the way, but then I realized that I was not at fault. I blamed myself for giving him so much love, but then, I didn't realize that he was battling his own demons. He was battling past childhood trauma—his mother was an addict while his father wasn't really involved in his life. In turn, he became an alcoholic and started to hate his existence on earth. I didn't abandon him—some women would, but I didn't. After all, he was still my husband and the father of my children. I made myself available to him, and I took care of him the best way a wife could. I showed him the love and care he deserved. When your loved one or spouse goes through trauma, the best way to deal with it is to show them all the love in the world and make them believe that they still have a purpose here on earth. Make them believe in love again. Love and the actions you take can heal wounds.

Many of us resort to shutting ourselves off instead of getting up and going again. We engage in self-destructive habits that will leave us in a worse state. Because I passed through something similar, I connected with him deeply. I understood what he was going through and used my story as a constant reminder that he was never alone in this world. Did it work? Yes. When you are going through a difficult time, it's not enough to shut yourself off and wallow in the pain. Seek out the words and company of those who understand what you are going through. You don't have to know them personally. You can read up on their stories in magazines and blogs. Cherish the wisdom they've gleaned, and use it to remind yourself that you can pull through. This is what I did for my husband, and thank Goodness, he pulled through.

Loving yourself will heal your wounds, no matter how deep they are. On the flip side, not doing that will open up your heart and soul to accepting hate, and you can remain broken for a long time. As a life coach, I've seen several people recover their lives after being broken. They didn't do this based on a magic formula. They simply imbibed self-love and did the things that would put them back on the right track. I usually tell people that they are in charge of their own destiny. The past is nothing more than a story that we repeat to ourselves. While it's impossible to forget because they are all pieces that form the puzzle, you should allow yourself time to understand these events and use them to influence yourself positively. Learn from the destruction of your past, and then move forward with those lessons learned.

Now that you know the value of self-love and how it can help you to heal, how do you practice it? These are the steps you should take.

Control Your Timing

Determine how you spend your time. Discard any tangible activity that doesn't produce any result. You don't need to spend time extravagantly because time is precious, especially regarding your healing. What are the things that are important in your life? Take this opportunity to declutter your schedule. Make a list of the things that you do and write down how much time you want to spend on each activity. Cut down on unnecessary activities by crossing them off on your list. You can only heal by making good use of your time and doing those productive things that will make you heal faster.

Awake as the sun rises and use this time to reflect and meditate. Reflections and meditation are essential to help keep the mind and body at ease. It deepens the connection between the mind and body, and this fosters healing. Rather than waking up to visit your social media profiles or check your emails, start the day with meditation. After that, do those activities that you have written down on your list.

Get in Shape

Most people go to the gym only to make their appearance appealing, but is that your perspective? Rather than focusing on what your workout does to the outward body, concentrate on how it makes you feel— how it affects your mindset, strength, and ability to focus on life's goals. Harness its power and use it to remind yourself that you are much more than capable of doing anything to achieve success. Exercise does so much more to the mind than it does to the physical body.

Take Some Time Off

In my 30s, I traveled a lot with my husband and children, not for fun but because we saw it as a way to escape our usual surroundings and see the world outside our doorstep. We usually took a week for our vacation, and this helped my husband and me recover from the pain that had happened in our lives, particularly his battle through childhood trauma and alcoholism.

A change in scenery is powerful, and sometimes we underestimate its significance. A new environment can lead to a change in mindset. Being away from home allows you the freedom to think and observe the world in another view. It gives you the tranquility to heal on your own terms. Spending more time in nature or outdoors will give you a clear mind, and this can restore positive energy.

Take some time out and spend it on the road or outdoors, somewhere far from your home and away from social media notifications. Disconnecting from your everyday life will make you realize how insignificant most of your worries and pains are and how you can completely thrive outside of them.

Strengthen Your Relationships with People Who Are There for You

The sad events and circumstances my husband and I went through strengthened our relationship even more deeply, and instead of going through a divorce, we decided to remain a family. When everything is falling apart, take notice of the people that are standing by you. Think back to times when life was about to hang you dry. Who were the people that stood beside you? Those are the ones that matter the most. Take note of them and appreciate them for their support.

Allow New People into Your Life

The positive effects of having people around you are immeasurable, and sometimes this might be the only way to heal yourself of all the trauma and negativity that's happened in your life. The fact is we all think, behave, and act like the people we spend most of our time around, and our quality of life is often a reflection of these same people. If those around you are toxic and negatively influence you, it's high time that you cut them loose and build stronger relationships with the ones who make you feel like a better version of yourself. If you surround yourself with positive people, you will heal faster and find it easier to move forward.

Be Disciplined About Self-Care

Emotional struggle is no different from being sick. When you are sick, you get plenty of rest, drink fluids, and take medicine. When you are going through an emotional phase, you have to make self-care a priority. This allows you to recover quickly and go through a less painful recovery. I focused more on myself during my recovery phase, and that did sure make my recovery quicker than expected. All you have to do is pay more attention to what your body and mind need and try all that you can to satisfy them.

Alter Your Appearance

Sometimes, the best way to heal yourself and overcome emotional trauma is to deliberately make a change to your outward appearance. Your outward appearance is a reflection of your internal self. By changing your hair or your dress, you are bringing change into your life.

Walk Away When You Can

Undoubtedly, one of the single most important steps to healing yourself from the pains of yesterday is to walk away from situations that hold you back. A lot of us are involved in a toxic relationship, such as doing a job that we have no passion for. It doesn't pay you to remain in terrible situations like this. You can start over, and to do that, you need to walk away from what makes you miserable.

It takes an exceptional amount of courage to break away from what you've known and carried in your heart all this while, but remember, you have got the absolute power to decide how you want to live your life and who you want to become. This gives you the opportunity to start over in the way you have always wanted to.

Healthy Eating

Putting the right foods into our bodies is one of the key things that can help our bodies to heal, physically and mentally. A healthy diet can boost our energy levels and state of the mind and restore balance in our body. Eat the right amount of fruits and veggies daily. Make a healthy diet plan containing grains, vegetables, protein, and fruits.

Adding vitamins to your diet plan is also good practice. Vitamin supplements reduces stress and play a tremendous role in how our bodies recover from painful past experiences. You will notice how much better you feel and your energy level will improve. Try to get some vitamin supplements if you can.

Learn Something New

Sometimes, the only way we can declutter our minds and let go of harmful memories is to replace them with new thoughts. Our mental landscape changes according to what we know. By learning new things, you are expanding the database of your knowledge and learning different views of the world.

What can you learn? You can pick up a new language. I always advise people struggling to deal with relationships or past experiences to learn a language. Do you know why? Learning a new language exposes you to the culture of the native speakers. You remind yourself that there's more world out there that you are yet to explore, one that operates on a different sense of the serene than yours. Learning that language and that serenity proves that you can adapt to one of those realities. This helps you to heal faster.

There are always new things to learn, so find that thing you are passionate about or have always wanted to learn and go for it.

Challenge Yourself

What makes a person successful is their ability to overcome their fears and stand up to life's challenges. This boosts their confidence and makes them stronger. As you undergo the healing phase, make it a point to challenge yourself in various ways. Take on that challenge that has always scared you. The strength that will come from conquering your fears and bad habits will take you further and hasten your healing process.

Be Mindful of Trauma Bonding & Social Vices

Life experiences that have been traumatizing can make you resort to trauma bonding and the use of social vices like drug/alcohol addiction, illicit sexual activities, and even hurting others. These can prolong your healing process. No matter the therapy or process you are using to heal yourself of yesterday's pain, if you stick to engaging in evil or bad habits like drug addiction, you are taking two steps backward. Your health will be affected, and surely, your judgment and decisions will be clouded. One of the reasons it feels impossible to quit this lifestyle is the circle of friends that you keep. You can only attract the wrong people if you are doing the wrong things. Friends can be destructive and helpful simultaneously.

So while you have made up your mind to quit these vices, filter the friends around you. The good people around you can help you recover from your traumatic experiences.

The healing process and how you recover from your past depend on you. The only way to heal is to love yourself first. A parent that loves their child will do everything to keep their son or daughter from danger. The same thing applies to you. If you love yourself, you will avoid doing anything that will keep you locked up in pain and sad circumstances.

Pain - Power - Purpose

Chapter Eight

LIGHTS, NO CAMERA, ONLY ACTION

"The way to develop decisiveness is to start right where you are, with the very next question you face."
—Napoleon Hill

There are twenty-four hours in a day, and I'm pretty sure that you want to make the most of them. The only thing that would make this possible is to be more decisive. Being decisive will prevent you from going back and forth on a topic. However, for many people, making decisions is tough. They would want to think carefully about their approach so that only the best decision would be made. While this is valid thinking, spending too much time contemplating before making a decision is the reason many people fail to actually make the decision. You could be a lot faster, and all you have to do is just decide. Only Action!

How can you make decisions faster? First off, don't make the decision when you feel pressured or distracted by too many things. Look for a moment when you are less busy and have more time to make a choice. There are instances when you need to make a decision on the spot. When it comes to that, buy yourself some time to think before deciding. Typically, people who are indecisive and find themselves going back and forth on big decisions often struggle to make decisions on little things as well. Harness the ability to decide by committing to everyday practice. You can give yourself 30 seconds to decide on what movie to watch, what food to cook for dinner, and the like. Work on this more consistently, and in no time, you will be making bigger decisions easily.

When you decide to forgive someone or forget an incident that makes you to feel sad without overanalyzing, you are making a bold statement. It means that you have overcome your fear of holding on. Deciding is a skill that takes a lot of commitment and effort, and sometimes, making that single decision can change your entire life for good. But when you second-guess whether to forgive or not, you are backing away from making a decision. This can affect you adversely.

Some decisions can leave you worse off, and you may begin to regret why you came to your conclusion in the first place. Not all of your decisions and actions will be perfect. Instead of beating yourself up about it, it's okay to joke about making that decision and learn from it. Learn to accept the consequences of your decisions and move on. Maybe if you had not made that decision, you could have been more successful now. Maybe if you had made that decision quickly, you wouldn't have lost your loved one to suicide. Learn to take action, and don't allow your fears and uncertainty to interfere.

Pain - Power - Purpose

Purpose

Pain - Power - Purpose

Chapter Nine

THE PURPOSE

> *"If you can't figure out your purpose,*
> *figure out your passion.*
> *For your passion will lead you right*
> *into your purpose"*
> —Bishop T.D. Jakes

What's your purpose in life? Have you even discovered your mission on earth and why you were created? Looking back, I never imagined that I would come this far in my life. My past was nothing close to fun or exciting. It was more of a misadventure—a journey of pain, misery, and trauma. I was raised by a single, alcoholic mother, grandparents, and great-grandparents, with my father in and out of my life. I started taking care of my brother at the age of nine and started working at the age of fourteen. I didn't enjoy the benefits children growing up with both parents did, and I thought life was just being unfair to me. I was miserable, and I quit jobs partly because I didn't find fulfilment in them, but it was really the triggers of my co-workers that brought out my trauma.

However, I never realized that it was preparing me for the future and a bigger mission. The trials and tribulations were set by God to make me stronger and better prepared for life's challenges. I didn't discover this until I was in my late twenties. Then, my relationship with God improved, and I began to understand that every single event and circumstance that happens in one's life is predestined. Now, I live happily with my wonderful husband and our four wonderful, beautiful children.

Everything in life happens for a reason. Sometimes, we may be too distracted or ignorant to understand, but every event teaches you a lesson and makes you stronger. My relationship with God improved after certain incidents happened in my life. If my husband didn't battle past childhood trauma when we had our fourth child or when he cheated on me, maybe our marriage wouldn't have been stronger—maybe I wouldn't be here writing a book or helping others through their trauma. My life's purpose consists of everything that motivates me to get up in the morning—everything I went through in life.

Now, back to the question: what's your life's purpose, and why is it essential that you discover it? A lot of people wake up in the morning not knowing where to go, what to do, or how to live their life. Others wake up each morning feeling that they have a lot to accomplish, and in the evening, they go to bed feeling fulfilled and satisfied. The difference between the first group of people and the second is that the latter utilizes their gifts and passions to make the day productive. That is why they retired for the night, feeling happy and less stress. Are you part of the first or second group? According to a poll by International Gallup, less than 20% of people interviewed enjoyed their job. These people also described themselves as engaged with their work and felt happier than those who felt disengaged.

Purpose can guide your life's decisions, shape your goals, and offer a sense of direction. People give different meaning to purpose though. To some, it lies in their vocation and the satisfaction they get from doing it. According to Fredrick Buechner, vocation is where our greatest passion meets the world's greatest need. This means that our job is not only a source of income but interwoven with our life's purpose. To others, purpose is all about utilizing your natural gifts and skills. We all possess different skills and gifts. Gifts are what make us feel fulfilled. For instance, making people feel happy with your comic skills is a gift. Others define their life's purpose as their responsibilities to their family and friends.

Some people find their purpose clearly expressed, while others don't know yet what their life's purpose is. Purpose is unique for everyone, and what you identify as your life's purpose may be different from others'. Also, your purpose can change as you go through different phases in your life. Your purpose shifts as your experience does. What does this mean? It means it's possible to have more than one purpose in life.

While you reflect on what your life's purposes are, there are specific questions that will come up, such as "Who am I?", "Where do I belong?", "When do I feel fulfilled?" and "What are my gifts and passions?" A friend of mine, Jenny, worked in the service industry traveling across the country. She liked the work she was doing, and the fact that the job paid her handsomely. However, her real love was caring for animals. As kids I can remember visiting her house; she had rabbits, birds, and dogs as pets. She would talk to them, nurture them and do whatever she could to help them when they were in distress. Her love for animals led her to study to become a veterinary nurse. Her passion has allowed her to travel and care for animals across the country. Jenny's life purposes were two—one was her profession, and the other was her gift to care for animals.. Fortunately, she derived joy from both.

Few things are sadder than watching a person with so much potential waste their life without utilizing their gifts. Many of us have gifts that we aren't fully expressing. It may be that we don't know they exist. Sometimes, we don't even know that we use them. They come so effortlessly and frequently that we overlook and take them for granted. How do you know that you have a gift? Ask yourself what you are good at and love to do. You will be able to identify your gifts from the responses to these questions. If you have a long list of what you are good at, look out for those ones that you enjoy doing with ease and pleasure.

Your passions work in accordance with your gift is the driving force of your gift. It's your passion that will reveal where you want to direct your energy and your gift to achieve your goals. How do you identify your passion? Ask yourself what you care about the most in the world and whom you want to help the most. Do you feel engaged with what you are doing? When your life and work choices are based on your gifts and passions, your purpose emerges. Don't forget that your values also play a big part in the equation. Your values support your actions, and they are the driving force of your decisions. Your values can be caring for others with kindness, treating others equally, and such.

Many people feel hesitant about pursuing their life's purpose because they worry it's a selfish quest. But true purpose is about recognizing your talents and using them to contribute to the world. According to Richard Leider, the formula for purpose is:

Talent + passion + values = purpose.

Questioning your life purpose usually arise when you are at crossroads. That is, when you are in a storm or a moment of transition. For instance, a rough past, marital challenges, personal loss, or change in career. I discovered my life's purpose during my marital crisis. If you are going through a difficult moment, it may be God telling you that your life's purpose lies within that crisis.

It's important to note that your life's purpose evolves. As we grow and experience life in different ways, new possibilities emerge, and our life's purpose begins to adapt too. Sometimes, it's during this period that we experience chaos, and then we begin to ask questions. It's perfectly normal.

WHY IS LIFE PURPOSE IMPORTANT?

There are moments when you may experience true connection with what you are doing. At other times, you may feel disconnected with what you are doing, and it's almost as if you are being forced to do it. The fact is that whatever you are doing that doesn't make you happy and feel connected isn't in harmony with your life purpose. When you are fulfilling your life purpose, you feel authentic, content, alive, and in a state of total absorption. You feel absolute satisfaction. This is what purpose is supposed to be—it offers emotional, physical, and psychological benefits.

Having a Strong Sense of Purpose Leads to Better Relationships

People with more purpose tend to be more engaged with others and find joy in associating with them. They understand why they get along in a relationship or want to associate with these individuals in the first place. They value each person and understand the other's strengths and weaknesses to some extent. As a result, relationships become stronger and everyone encourages each other to live at peace with one another. They tend to enjoy better relationships because they choose their associates or friends consciously. They know whom they need to be close to and whom they need to distance themselves from. After all, they understand the purpose of every relationship.

You Become More Resilient When You Have a Strong Sense of Purpose

One characteristic of people who live with purpose is that they can find meaning in the events that happen to them. These people are able to reappraise situations, condition their emotions, and solve their life's issues. Having purpose makes you insusceptible to pain. You can handle the ups and downs of life without being negatively affected. Purpose offers a psychological buffer against depression, anxiety, and obstacles. Such a person remains satisfied with life, even when they are experiencing a difficult day. This type of resilience can also act as a buffer against long-term diseases and health issues.

HOW TO LIVE A PURPOSEFUL LIFE

Living a purposeful life is possible, and you can do that day to day. You need to engage in two core practices—contemplation and activation. Contemplation is seeking answers to questions about your existence on earth, how you should live, and where you belong. To help you answer these questions, try some reflective practices, journaling, or meditation. These will help the mind to relax and redirect your focus to the present moment.

How do you reflect? Review the day's events chronologically for five to ten minutes each evening. Reflect upon where you have been, the events that affected you positively, and the obstacles that you encountered. Ask yourself whether you were able to overcome the issues that arose, and most importantly, ask yourself what lessons you gained and what experiences were energy-draining. Finding answers to these questions will help you to live a more purposeful life. Take this period of the day to examine whether you felt alive and experienced some flow doing those activities. Cut out those activities and experiences that were draining and focus on the ones that made you feel alive and needed.

How does journaling help in making your life more purposeful? Keeping a journal allows you to express yourself honestly in ways that you won't be able to using other mediums. Write freely without stopping to edit, and allow your emotions to flow, detailing all your experiences. If you can, set a timer to remember when to write and keep your notepad in an accessible place, like beside your bed, so that you won't have issues finding an opportunity to write. If you remember any dreams, record them when you wake up. Dreams are a way for the mind to work on matters that people may or may not acknowledge consciously. Some dreams are prophetic, or rather, parabolic, and they can provide accurate insights into your needs.

How do you meditate? It's best to do this in the early hours of the morning, shortly after the sunrise. Sit down for ten to twenty minutes each day and only observe the environment. Allow your mind to wander freely. Consistent practice will help you to live purposefully day to day.

After contemplation, your next focus is activation—taking what you have realized about yourself truthfully and acting upon it. At this stage you are creating an authentic life for yourself, that is, syncing your inner self to match your outer self. When you start to align your everyday life with those fulfilling moments, you are able to live a purposeful life.

TIPS FOR FINDING YOUR PURPOSE IN LIFE

As discussed so far, living your best life depends on whether you have found your purpose. The combination of a loving family, strong network of friends, and a successful career may seem like the ideal life. However, even those who check all the boxes realize that something is missing. That thing is their purpose in life.

It's what you derive joy from and what drives you to live a healthier, better life. Now that you understand how to live a purposeful life by reflecting and meditating, cultivating the seven habits below will also help you live a healthier, better life.

Volunteer and Help Others

Helping others creates a kind of inner satisfaction that's almost inexplicable. By being a giver, helping others, and volunteering, you are adding value to other people's lives, which makes you feel as though your own life is more meaningful. You may be the reason why some people haven't given up hope for a better tomorrow, the light they expect to see at the end of the tunnel. Volunteering to help others is a beautiful gesture that not only brings you inner satisfaction but also makes the world a better place to live in.

Listen to Feedback

Sometimes, it can be difficult to know the things you are passionate about. You may even be passionate about a lot of things, and these become so ingrained in your life that you don't know how important they are. Fortunately, there are people who might be able to give you some direction. If you don't get any feedback, you can reach out to people and ask them what they think. Write down the compliments you receive and look for the patterns in them. Hearing what other people think about your passion may be will reignite it and make you redirect your focus.

Surround Yourself with Positive People

You are the reflection of the people you roll with. Do your friends influence you positively or negatively? Do you feel good, energized, and inspired when you are in the company of your friends? If you are surrounded with people who impact you positively, you will feel happy and be passionate about helping contribute to others' lives.

Meet and Talk with New People

When you have extra time strolling your neighborhood or walking the aisle of the grocery store, take the time to talk to the people around you. Start up a friendly conversation with people and learn what's up with them. Find out how they are doing, whether they are working on any project, or what they like to do for fun. At first, it might look as if you are poking your nose in other people's business, even being awkward talking to strangers, but maintaining a friendly face is the first step in getting their attention. Talking to people outside your circle will open your eyes to new possibilities and career opportunities that you never knew existed.

ENJOY THE PRESENT

Take the time to enjoy what you are doing in the moment. The past is behind you. Enjoy the presence of people, places and things surrounding you, now. Tomorrow is not promised and living with regrets is not what you want in this lifetime. Be present!

WAYS TO KNOW WHEN YOU HAVE FOUND YOUR PURPOSE

Finding a purpose is a little bit similar to someone finding inspiration. Sometimes, you just know that you got it, but for others, it can be difficult to tell whether they have found their life's purpose or not. You lose it right after you stop looking for it. Let's check out ways to know that you've found your life's purpose.

What You Are Doing Feels Like It's Part of You

Knowing that you have found a purpose may be difficult at times because you may face obstacles that will deflect your mind from thinking that you have found it. However, there are clues to know that you have found your purpose. One is that you will feel great and comfortable doing certain tasks. It's like imagining how your life would look, as if you were daydreaming. That's exactly what finding your purpose will be like. It will seem as if you have arrived and that you were always supposed to be there. That it's just meant for you alone.

You Have More Energy

When you find your purpose, you don't mind pursuing it 24/7. You never tire of it because it's something that you love doing. Maybe you are making a difference in the lives of couples like I do, helping them move through their traumatic past. Or maybe you are making a difference in the lives of children or the vulnerable. No matter what you do and how long you have been doing it, you just don't feel tired. In fact, chances are that you are working harder than before, but you still feel more fulfilled and energetic after it. When you come home at night, you don't feel stressed, but like you have been resting at home all day. You just jump into bed feeling happy and wake up with more energy to carry you through the next day's work. Finding your purpose is hardly different from falling in love.

Other People's Lives Are Enriched by What You Are Doing

A popular belief is that pursuing your purpose is really doing something for your own selfish gain. However, this idea doesn't apply to everything. Like every rule, there are always exceptions. For the most part, when you discover your true purpose, other people's lives will be impacted positively by what you are doing. They will recognize it almost instantly because they love what you are doing and how they're benefitting from it. When you see this, you will be even more exited to share your purpose and give yourself to the service and needs of the people. Remember, finding your purpose might be serving others with your passions and gift. This is just it. You'll also be happy to help others discover their life's purpose. In the end, your life wouldn't be the only one that will change—you would change the lives of others as well.

It's No Longer About the Money

Once you've found your true purpose, money will no longer be the only reason you do what you do. You will be willing to accept a pay cut when a financial obstacle arises. In fact, you may think of coming up with ways to get money just to continue doing what you love. You will just make it happen somehow. Once you know what your purpose is, money will only become a trivial topic.

You Are Willing to Take Risks and Are No Longer Scared

Just like how money will become the least talked about topic, you will be willing to take risks and will no longer be scared of going out there to prove your worth. You will become your own kind god, and won't need anyone to tell you what a wonderful job you are doing. You will be willing to go all out to succeed, and you will become absolutely sure that everything will work out fine.

You Feel that You Have Been Prepared All Your Life

Once you have realized your purpose, you will see a pattern of preparation in your past. You will feel that you have been training all your life for that day. This is something most people say when they are happy with their progress. Those who feel that they are doing what they aren't supposed to do have a tendency to be on a never-ending journey to the promised land. These are the kind of people that hop from job to job or move from one business to the other. But one thing about finding a purpose is it doesn't start spontaneously—at the time, you may not have even known that what you were doing was preparing you for the future, but somehow, in the present, you now find happiness in what you are doing. Now when you look back, you realize that all your efforts weren't in vain.

Other People with a Similar Purpose Find their Way into Your Life

Once you have found your purpose, people with similar life purpose will be attracted to you. Call it the Law of Attraction. You will be automatically introduced to people who are looking for what you offer. All you have to do is embrace every person that runs into you with a similar purpose. Don't question it. It's the Law of Attraction that's at work here.

A Community Will Find You

You may discover that what you do has been widely broadcasted without you even knowing it. Communities will start to notice you and start to seek you out for solutions and advice. They just want you to make them feel happy and good about their lives. Inside, you will feel extremely happy to help them. Additionally, the communities will want to see you succeed and want what's best for you.

You Will Feel Peaceful Even with the Stress

When you finally discover your life's purpose, you will feel more at ease with yourself. Even when life's pressure and challenges begin to mount on you, you will still feel settled within your soul. Life will seem oddly peaceful because you already know what you are supposed to be doing every time. It's like being on cloud nine.

You Will Become a Better Version of Yourself

Finding your purpose isn't just about making people feel good or being fulfilled. You also become a better version of yourself because you see the world in a better way and the people living in it as great and loving. With each new day that passes, as the sun shines brighter, your level of happiness remains the same. The world didn't change you or make you believe so, the changes started inside of you, and being the light that you are, you begin to illuminate the world. The world becomes a reflection of your values and everything you stand for.

Your Relationships with People Improves Despite What Life Throws at You

Finding your purpose puts you in a position to meet different people. Your purpose helps you realize your duty to others around you, which in turn improves your relationships.

Sometimes on your road to finding your purpose, some people may call you "terrible," and to an extent, label you "selfish." It's not their fault, neither is it yours—you are on a journey of self-discovery, so it's expected that you may wrong one or two people. Now that you have found your purpose, it's time to make amends, drop all the negativity, and show more love. Your purpose will strengthen your relationship.

If you haven't found your purpose yet, that doesn't mean it doesn't exist. Millions of other people in the world are in a similar situation. What you need to do now is to keep your heart open and to keep looking. Continue to explore opportunities, and one day, you will find your purpose.

ACKNOWLEDGEMENTS

First and foremost, thank you God, the Divine Creator for your grace and mercy.

I would like to express a deep sense of gratitude to my husband, children, teachers, and my former students that I came across in my years of existence. This project wouldn't have been completed without you all in my life. This book is a reflection of all your input, and I will never forget all the words of encouragement you offered during the writing of my book.

I also want to thank my parents, grandparents, and my late great-grandparents for my upbringing.

Special thanks go to our late pastor and counselor for being there for me and for my family when it mattered the most.

To all my family, friends, and co-workers, I would like to say a big thank you for all the love and prayer you showered on me.

To the person reading this book, I thank you and wish you many blessings on your journey.

Made in the USA
Middletown, DE
10 February 2022